Christian Meditation

Your Daily Practice

Christian Meditation

Your Daily Practice

Laurence Freeman, OSB

NOVALIS / MEDIO MEDIA

This edition of *Christian Meditation: Your Daily Practice*
is published by Novalis under license from Medio Media.
First published by Hunt & Thorpe, 1994.

Cover design: Christiane Lemire
Cover photograph: ImagePack
Layout: Les éditions Multi
The portrait of John Main on page 27
was painted by Brenda Bury.

Publishing Office
10 Lower Spadina Avenue, Suite 400
Toronto, Ontario, Canada
M5V 2Z2

Head Office
4475 Frontenac Street
Montréal, Québec, Canada
H2H 2S2

www.novalis.ca

ISBN-13 978-2-89088-855-5

Medio Media
627 N 6th Ave., Tucson, Arizona
85705 (USA)
(520) 882-0290
1-800-324-8305

Reprint 2011

Printed in Canada.

We acknowledge the financial support of the Government of Canada
through the Canada Book Fund for business development activities.

Contents

Introduction

This little book originated in the need to express the essentials of meditation in the Christian tradition for people leading weekly meditation groups in our world-wide community of Christian meditation. But because these essentials are so simple – simplicity itself – the book can serve equally well as an introduction to meditation for anyone wishing to deepen his spiritual life.

These essentials are practical. I hope they can help you to open up a richer dimension of consciousness in your ordinary life by undertaking the simple daily practice of silence and stillness.

Meditation is simple. That is why it so easily becomes complicated. This book suggests a way of understanding and of undertaking such a simple path for people who are likely to have basic questions and who may even have been led to think that meditation is complex and difficult.

If we can be encouraged actually to meditate, rather than just think about it, the questions begin to be answered, and simplified, by the experience itself. Any book, talk, or course on meditation is valuable only if it leads directly to the threshold of the experience of silence. These six chapters can be read as a whole and also used as part of a series of introductory talks for meditation groups or adapted to a single introductory talk. Personal witness and the authenticity of personal conviction are essential elements in any spiritual communication. But above all, we teach meditation primarily by meditating with people.

The further reading list at the end of the book provides a resource to broaden your introduction to meditation in the Christian tradition. Practice will show how meditation, within any tradition, becomes a bridge of peace and unity, and how it overcomes all barriers and every kind of resistance to the "abundant life" promised by Jesus.

Laurence Freeman, OSB
The World Community
for Christian Meditation

1

What Is Prayer?

A very old definition of prayer described it as "the raising of the heart *and* mind to God." What is the "mind," what is the "heart"? The mind is what thinks – it questions, plans, worries, fantasizes. The heart is what knows – it loves. The mind is the organ of knowledge, the heart, the organ of love. Mental consciousness must eventually give way and open up to the fuller way of knowing which is heart consciousness. Love is complete knowledge.

Most of our training in prayer, however, is limited to the mind. We were taught as children to say our prayers, to ask God for what we or others need. But this is only half of the mystery of prayer.

The other half is the prayer of the heart where we are not thinking of God or talking to him or asking for anything. We are simply being with God who is in us in the Holy Spirit whom

Jesus has given us. The Holy Spirit is the love, the relationship of love that flows between Father and Son. It is this Spirit Jesus has breathed into every human heart. Meditation, then, is the prayer of the heart uniting us with the human consciousness of Jesus in the Spirit.

> We do not even know how to pray but the Spirit himself prays *within us*.

Romans 8:26

For mental prayer – praying in words or using thoughts about God – we can make rules. There are many "methods of mental prayer," but for the prayer of the heart there is no technique, no rules: "Where the Spirit is, there is liberty" (2 Corinthians 3:17).

The Holy Spirit in the modern Church, especially since the Vatican Council in the early 1960's, has been teaching us to recover this other dimension of our prayer. The Council documents on the Church and the liturgy both emphasized the need to develop "a contemplative orientation" in the spiritual life of Christians today. All are called to the fullness of the experience of Christ, whatever their way of life.

This means that we must move beyond the level of mental prayer: talking to God, thinking about God, asking God for our needs. We must go to the depths, to where the spirit of Jesus himself is praying in our hearts, in the deep silence of his union with our Father in the Holy Spirit.

Contemplative prayer is not the privilege of monks and nuns or special mystical types. It is a dimension of prayer to which we are called. It is not about extraordinary experiences or altered states of consciousness. It is what Thomas Aquinas called the "simple enjoyment of the truth." William Blake spoke of the need to "cleanse the doors of perception" so that we can see everything as it truly is: infinite.

This is all about the contemplative consciousness as lived in ordinary life. Meditation leads us to this and it is part of the whole mystery of prayer in the life of any person who is seeking fullness of being.

Think of prayer as a great wheel:

The wheel turns our whole life towards God. Prayer is an essential part of a fully human life. If we do not pray, we are only half-alive and our faith is only half-developed.

The spokes of the wheel represent the different types of prayer. We pray in different ways, at different times, and according to how we feel. Different people have preferred ways of prayer. The spokes represent, for example, the Eucharist, the other sacraments, spiritual prayer, petitionary and intercessory prayer, charismatic prayer, devotions, the rosary, etc.

But what makes all these different forms of prayer Christian is that they are centred in Christ. The spokes are the forms or expressions of prayer which fit into the hub of the wheel which is the prayer of Jesus himself.

His prayer is the essential meaning and source of a Christian's prayer. We could paraphrase St. Paul: I pray no longer but Christ prays in me. So, in this model of the wheel, all forms of prayer flow into and out of the spirit of Jesus worshipping God in and on behalf of creation. All forms of prayer are valid. All are effective. They are informed by the prayer of the human consciousness of Jesus which is in us by the grace of the Holy Spirit.

This is a faith understanding of the wheel of prayer. We are not thinking about all this at the time of meditation itself. Experientially, the wheel teaches us something of great importance as well. At the hub of the wheel, at the centre of prayer, you find stillness. Without stillness at the centre, there could be no movement or growth at the circumference. Meditation is the work of finding and becoming one with this stillness, which is the hallmark of the Spirit. "Be still and know that I am God!"

Contemplative prayer is total openness to and oneness with the prayer of Jesus. Contemplation is being silent, still and simple. And the heart of the prayer of Jesus is his communion of love with the Father, his turning his attention to the Father, in the Holy Spirit.

Christian prayer, therefore, means entering the life of the Holy Trinity in, through and with the human mind and heart of Jesus.

For many people, prayer is basically an appeal to God for special help in particular times of distress. It is natural to express our faith and trust in God in this way and at such times. But what is our faith in God? Is it not that, as Jesus says, God knows our needs before we ask?

We do not express our needs to God either to inform God of what he does not know or to persuade God to change his mind. If we do pray for our needs, it is above all because doing so deepens our trust that God knows and God cares.

Unless this faith is clear and deep, our prayer can easily be bogged down in an arrested stage of development, stuck at the level of the ego. For many Christians this is the crisis of their faith today, and it reflects the often shallow level of Christian spirituality.

The prayer of the heart, contemplative prayer, meditation, is essentially the prayer of faith. In silence we accept that God knows our needs and that this knowledge is the love which creates and will eventually complete us.

If this helps to answer the question "What is prayer?" the next question is "How do we pray?" Only by praying can we actually discover what prayer means and that prayer must occupy the heart of any really meaningful life.

2

How Do We Pray?

St. Paul said that we do not know how to pray, but the Spirit prays within us (Romans 8:26). This is the key to understanding the real meaning of Christian prayer. It suggests that we learn to pray not by trying to pray, but by giving up, or letting go, of our trying. And instead, learning to be.

This opens access to the deeper prayer of the heart where we can find the "love of God flooding our inmost heart through the Holy Spirit he has given us" (Romans 6:5). This is pure experience, beyond thought, dogma and imagination.

The important question is how can we open our whole self to this pure experience of love in our "inmost being"? First, let's look at the three essential elements of contemplation again. These answer the question "how" do we pray – we pray by becoming silent, still and simple.

1. Silence

We need silence for our psychological health as well as for our spiritual growth. With television, personal stereos and the traffic noise in modern cities, silence is becoming more and more difficult to experience.

But the real silence is interior. In fact, even if we are in a very noisy place, we can be silent if we are concentrated, which means at one with our own centre. We learn to be silent by paying attention. Attention brings the centre of our being to full consciousness. It brings us from the past and the future into the present which is gentle and restful.

There is no reason why we cannot be silent in a busy street, in a traffic jam, or waiting in a supermarket line. Learning to be silent at the times of meditation teaches us to "pray" at all times. It teaches us also to use every delay or frustration in daily life as an opportunity, indeed a gift, to go deeper, to learn to listen, to wait in our new-found silence.

Silence is truthful. It is healing. It pacifies our inner turmoil. It is the cure for destructive anger, anxiety and bitterness.

In silence we learn the universal language of the Spirit. God speaks the creative word out of a boundless silence which pervades all we think and do.

Silence in prayer, as between two people, is a sign of trust and acceptance. Without the capacity to be silent, we are unable to listen to another person. In its essence, silence is nothing less than worship in spirit and truth.

So, it is not just the absence of noise. Silence is a whole attitude of being, of relating, and an openness to the mutual knowing and inter-being which is love.

2. Stillness

One of the psalms says "Be still and know that I am God" (Psalm 46:10). Stillness does not mean a state of inertia or death. To know God is to be fully alive.

Stillness is the balance of all the many forces and energies that make up a person – physical, mental and spiritual.

As with silence, stillness has both an exterior and an interior dimension. Stillness has nothing to do with the holding in, the blocking or the repression of movement or action. It is the fulfilment of all movement and action.

In prayer we need to come to physical stillness. This is the first step of the inner journey to God at the centre of our being. Physical stillness helps us to realize that our bodies are sacred – "temples of the Holy Spirit" (1 Corinthians 6:19).

In fact, simply learning to sit still is a great step forward on any spiritual path. For many it is the first lesson in going beyond desire – the urge to scratch or fidget. Our physical restlessness reflects not only bodily stress and tension, but also mental anxiety and distractedness. Physical stillness has a direct effect upon the silence of our mind, and so helps immensely to bring body, mind and spirit into harmony.

But the next dimension of stillness is interior. To come to a stillness of mind is the great challenge of prayer. How can we deal with the constant activity of the mind? Buddhists say the mind has 151 operations going on at the same time! Desires, dreams and great expectations can divide and dominate our mind.

3. Simplicity

Christian prayer is awakening to the reality that we are at home now in the kingdom of God. Jesus told us that the kingdom of God is within us and also that we must become like children, if we are to enter this kingdom. "The Kingdom is not a place but an experience" (John Main). Being simple is not easy. We are constantly analysing ourselves, our feelings, our motives – or other people's – and our constant self-consciousness makes us very complex and confused.

But God is simple – love is simple. Meditation is simple. Being simple means being ourselves. It means passing beyond self-consciousness, self-analysis and self-rejection.

Meditation is a universal spiritual practice which guides us into this state of prayer, into the prayer of Christ. It brings us to silence, stillness and simplicity by a means that is itself silent, still and simple.

The means is the repetition of a single sacred word faithfully and lovingly during the time of meditation. Today we call the sacred word a *mantra*. This is a very ancient Christian way of prayer which has been recovered for modern Christians by the Benedictine monk John Main (1926–1982).

John Main recovered this way of bringing the mind to rest in the heart through the teaching of the first Christian monks, the Desert Fathers, especially John Cassian (4th century A.D.). It is in the same tradition as the *Cloud of*

Unknowing written in England in the 14th
century.

John Main taught that to meditate you
1. sit still with your back straight
2. close your eyes
3. repeat your mantra interiorly, and
    continuously.

Choose a quiet time and place every
morning and evening and meditate for about
20–30 minutes each time.

An ideal mantra is the ancient Aramaic
phrase *maranatha*. Say it as four syllables of
equal length, clearly and continuously: MA-RA-
NA-THA. Say it without haste and without
expecting anything to happen. Listen to the
mantra with your whole being. Gently return to
it whenever you get distracted. Be simple. Be
faithful.

Aramaic is the language Jesus spoke, the
same language as the word "abba," which he
constantly used in referring to God. Maranatha
is the oldest Christian prayer. It means "Come
Lord," or "The Lord comes." St. Paul ends the
First Letter to the Corinthians, and St. John, the
Book of Revelation, with this phrase which
expresses the deep and simple faith of the early
church.

The meaning and sound of the word are both important. But as you say the word, do not think about the meaning. The mantra leads us deeper than thought, to pure being. It leads us by faith. We say the mantra in faith and love. Listening to the mantra as we say it is the ever-deepening work of a journey of faith.

Four rules help you to persevere:

- don't have any demands or expectations
- don't evaluate your meditation
- integrate it into your daily life, with morning and evening practice
- live its consequence, day by day.

3

The Christian Tradition of Meditation

As Christians, we meditate because we believe in the Risen Christ, that he lives and lives in us. As disciples of Jesus, the teacher, we have faith when he calls us to leave self behind and follow him into the kingdom of God, to "share in the very being of God."

It is our faith that makes our meditation Christian. It is also Christian because it is centred in the human consciousness of Jesus in our inmost being. As Christians, we naturally meditate with other Christians, and our lives are guided and enriched in community by Scripture, sacrament and all the different ways of ministering to others in the love and compassion of the Spirit.

The basic theology of meditation is the basic theology of the gospel. Jesus, by his life, death and resurrection, has opened up for us a way to

God, and by sending the Holy Spirit to us he has become our way and our guide.

Jesus did not teach any particular method of prayer, but we can see by what he says of prayer in the Sermon on the Mount, that meditation is a way to find him and to follow him. Meditation is wholly consistent with his teaching about prayer.

The Sermon on the Mount

1. Prayer, like good works, must not be merely outward. It is not about looking holy or winning other people's admiration. Nor is it even about feeling we are holy. Jesus says your "left hand must not know what your right is doing." Prayer is a humble and unselfconscious work which helps us to discern reality (Matthew 6:1-4).

2. Prayer must be interior. People who like their prayer to be too public easily fall into hypocrisy, which is discord between our inner and outer identity. Jesus tells us to go to "your private room" and pray in that "secret place." The word "secret" here also means "mysterious." Mystery is not magic. It is the experience of reality which mental consciousness by itself cannot contain or

understand. Prayer is by nature mysterious, and the deepest place of mystery in human life is the heart. The "private room" is a metaphor for the inner chamber of the heart (Matthew 6:5-6).

3. In prayer we must not "babble on." More words do not make God hear us better. Prayer is not about quantity – "prayers" – but about quality – "attention" (Matthew 6:7-8).

4. Prayer is not primarily about asking God for things because he "knows what we need before we ask him" (Matthew 6:8).

5. We must give priority to the spiritual treasures of the kingdom rather than material well-being (Matthew 6:19-21).

6. We must learn to stop worrying about the future and to trust in God. Anxiety is an enemy of prayer. It makes us too self-centred and prevents us from realizing the gift already deposited in love in our heart (Matthew 6:25-37).

7. Finally, Jesus says prayer is about "setting your mind on God's kingdom first." In other words, be attentive to the "one thing necessary" – be mindful. Then all the other

things will come to you as well (Matthew 6:33).

These seven teachings of Jesus on prayer are what we put into practice in meditation: humility, interiority, silence, trust, spirituality, peace and attention.

The Present Moment

Do not worry about tomorrow, he tells us. In meditation we stop thinking of the past and future and learn to live fully in the present moment.

Unfortunately, God often seems absent to us because we are not in the here and now. We spend much of our life locked into thoughts of the past and dreams of the future.

Thinking of the past breeds feelings of regret, nostalgia, melancholy or guilt. Living in the future quickly generates anxiety, fear and worry. The combination of moods which these feelings make does not add up to peace. Between past and future, which are constructs of the mind, you find the present moment which is absolute reality. The present moment – which is what we enter in meditation – is infinitely small – and therefore infinitely spacious.

The mantra clears a way through all the thoughts of past and future to reveal, in a thought-free state, the radiant reality of the here and now: the moment of Christ.

It is only in the present moment that we can find God, the God who calls himself "I AM."

Living in the present moment is an art that is practised in daily life. Ordinary life is the best school of meditation for this reason. It teaches the error of identifying God with religion, temple, synagogue, mosque or church, with pious language or with ritual. God is everywhere at all times. Meditation is the daily discipline that teaches us to see God in the here and now.

The contemplative experience is simply being fully conscious in the present moment. We do not have to master any difficult techniques or theories in order to meditate. We have only to be at home and to wake up. This is what the mantra helps us to do.

John Main
His Life and His Teaching

For many people around the world, John Main has been and remains an invaluable guide into a deeper spiritual life through his transmission of the Christian tradition of meditation. He saw meditation as a way to "accept the gift of one's being" as well as a way to "verify the truths of your faith." He was very insistent about our need to learn to be silent, and his own life reads as a kind of parable of the contemporary search for God. Bede Griffiths, a fellow Benedictine, said that, in his experience, John Main was the most important spiritual guide in Christianity today.

Introduction to Meditation

John Main was born in London in 1926 into a Catholic Irish family. After school he served in the front line in the closing stages of war. He then joined a religious order for about two years but left it to study law at Trinity College, Dublin. After graduation he entered the British Foreign Service and was posted to Malaya where he joined the Governor's staff and studied Chinese.

One day he was sent to visit a local Indian Hindu monk who ran an orphanage and ashram on the outskirts of Kuala Lumpur. After his official business was done, he fell into conversation on spiritual matters and soon sensed he was in the presence of a holy and enlightened man whose deep inner experience was the direct source of energy and inspiration for his works of compassion and reconciliation. From this monk, John Main learned a simple way of meditation: the faithful recitation of a mantra during two periods of meditation, before and after his day's work. Each week he would return to his teacher, meditate with him and be reinforced in his commitment to this discipline of silence, stillness and simplicity.

After returning to Europe to teach International Law for a number of years, John Main himself became a Benedictine monk in London. To his dismay, his novice master instructed him to give up his meditation because it was not a "Christian way of prayer." In his *Gethesemani Talks* John Main writes:

> In retrospect I regard this period of my life as a great grace. Unwittingly, my novice master had set out to teach me detachment at the very centre of my life. I learned to become detached from the practice that was most sacred to me and on which I was seeking to build my life. The next few years were bleak years in terms of spiritual development, but I think too there was a faith somewhere deep inside me that God would not leave me forever wandering in the wilderness and would lead me back on to the path. What was important was that I should come back on his terms and not on my own.
>
> (*Christian Meditation: The Gethsemani Talks*, p.15)

Some years later through his reading of the teachings of the early Christian monks, the Desert Mothers and Fathers, and in particular in the Conferences of John Cassian, he was led back on to the path. He discovered the Christian tradition of the mantra and went on to teach it from within the rich context of Christian Scripture and theology.

A Modern Tradition

He realized that in this simple and ancient tradition of prayer, modern people of all walks of life could find a spiritual daily discipline adaptable to their ordinary lives. And he sensed that the meeting of the great world religions could only be fulfilled if members of each faith approached each other from this depth of spiritual experience taught in their own tradition.

John Main's way of teaching reminds us of the oral tradition in which this way of contemplative wisdom has always been transmitted. His recorded talks continue to guide meditation groups each week around the world. He was a teacher who wished to lead others into their own experience, and he believed one could teach meditation only by meditating with people. The movement from thought to experience, theory to reality, mind to heart, is central to his vision of spiritual growth.

The greatest challenge of meditation for modern people, he said, is simplicity. We are trained to respect complexity. Yet simplicity is not easy to learn and, therefore, it requires discipline. Although he was insistent on the need to practise meditation as an interior and daily discipline, not just as a technique of self-enhancement, he also stressed the need for patience and gentleness in learning the discipline.

Essential Teachings

Meditation, he taught, is a way of self-knowledge and self-acceptance. This is the indispensable first step towards any knowledge of God. But it is not primarily an intellectual knowledge, for it is reached through a profound harmony of stillness in body and mind. The body itself is part of the journey to God. Nor is it an isolated or lonely journey. The solitude of meditation awakens us to our deep interdependence with other people and so "meditation creates community."

Community is how John Main saw the Church of the future. The spiritual renewal of Christianity is the next great step in its movement from mediaeval to modern identity. With this, there will come a new appreciation of the basic Christian understanding of prayer itself. Prayer is not talking or thinking about God but being with God. My prayer is not essentially mine at all if I am transcending my narrow egocentric view of reality. The essence of Christian prayer, he said, is the human consciousness of Jesus worshipping God in the Spirit at the centre of the human person.

He said he was not claiming that the mantra was the only way to this centre.

> I do not wish to imply that meditation is the only way, but rather that it is the only way that I have found. In my own experience it is the way of pure simplicity that enables us to become fully, integrally aware of the Spirit Jesus has sent into our heart; and this is the recorded experience of the mainstream of the Christian tradition from Apostolic times down to our own day.

(*Word into Silence*, p. 42)

John Main died in 1982 in a small community in Canada from which his teaching had begun to spread to many parts of the world. His work is now continued by the World

Community for Christian Meditation, which is a network of 25 Christian Meditation Centres and hundreds of groups meeting weekly around the world, and its International Centre in London. His books and taped talks are listed at the end of this book. An excellent picture of his life and personality is contained in *John Main by Those Who Knew Him* (edited by Paul Harris), and in a set of audio cassettes by Laurence Freeman called *John Main: His Life and Teaching*.

5

The Practice

Meditation is experiential. That is, it is a way of experience, rather than of theory or of thought at all. "Experience is the teacher," said John Cassian, who was John Main's inspiration for recovering this tradition of prayer for modern Christians.

The Body

Meditation is an incarnate way of prayer. The body is not a barrier between us and God. It is the sacrament of the gift of being which God has given us by creating us. It is a temple of the Holy Spirit of the risen Jesus.

That is why the body is part of the whole experience of prayer. We can discover this just by meditating. The simple rules are:

- sit down: the body is at rest but not in the usual position for sleep

- sit still: the body expresses the whole person's attitude of attention and reverence
- keep your back straight: the body is alert and wakeful
- breathe normally: ideally from the belly
- be relaxed but alert: the formula for peace.

When you first sit to meditate, take a while to find a posture you can be comfortable and steady in. Relax the obvious tensions of your body, in your shoulders, neck, eyes and forehead.

The basic sitting positions that you can try out are on a chair with a straight back, on a prayer stool, or sitting cross-legged on the floor with a small cushion beneath for support. The video *The Body at Prayer* gives helpful practical advice on all these positions. It is worth experimenting with them until you find the best one.

The yoga positions and breathing exercises are an excellent spiritual practice for the body. They will teach you reverence for your body as God's gift and temple. They are an ideal relaxing preparation for meditation.

Time and Place

Choose a quiet time and place where you are not likely to be distracted. Treat your meditation times as priority times. Put on the answering machine or unplug the phone.

You will come to see why meditators regard these times as the most important part of their day. If possible, keep to the same place and time each day as this helps deepen the rhythm of prayer in your life. But above all, be gentle with yourself. Take your time to insert this new discipline into your life. Remember that the word *discipline*, like the word *disciple*, comes from a root word meaning "to learn."

Early morning is best for the first period of meditation, before reading the newspaper or making phone calls. Early evening is best for the second period, after the day's work, before dinner and the activities of the evening.

The evening meditation is generally the most difficult to be faithful to. Do the best you can, but accept the inevitable if it happens you can't. But don't give up the regular second meditation of the day too easily. Look hard at your daily routine and make space for it. Why is it so often the busiest people who make time for meditation every day? The two daily periods give your day infinitely more than the hour they take from it. But only your own experience will convince you of this.

You can prepare for and conclude each meditation with some music or in any way that quietens and focuses you. And of course, meditation can be integrated with other ways of prayer, such as the Eucharist or Scripture.

Time your meditation in a regular and disciplined way. It is better to time it externally, for example, with a quiet beeper. Don't shorten or extend your time of meditation in a self-indulgent way, but be gentle about the self-discipline.

Meditation with a group each week is a powerful means of deepening your practice. You receive encouragement and inspiration from others, from hearing the essential teaching each week, and by entering into that dimension of the presence of Christ which is revealed "where two or three are gathered in my name" (Matthew 18:20). In time, you too will become able to share with others the gift you have received.

Distractions

The great practical difficulty all people find in meditation is the incessant problem of distraction. Don't be discouraged. All who have ever prayed, even the great masters of prayer, have experienced distractions. They are simply the effects of our constant mental activity. The mantra is the most simple and effective way to deal with all these kinds of thoughts.

1. Do not try to fight off the distractions, whether thoughts or images or feelings.

2. Give all your attention to the mantra, gently and faithfully returning to it all the way through your time of meditation.

3. Pay no attention to the distractions. Treat them as if they were background noise, like the noise of traffic outside.

4. Be humble, patient, faithful, and keep your sense of humour: don't make a dark night out of every cloud. But don't underestimate the perseverance you need and the grace you will be given.

The mantra is like a path through a thick jungle. However narrow the path may be, follow it faithfully and it will lead you out of the jungle of the mind into the great open space of the heart. Whenever you find you have wandered off the path, simply return to it straightaway.

The great gift of the mantra is its immediacy. However long you have been distracted, lost in the jungle of the mind, you are never more than one step away from the path. Start saying the mantra again, and you are back on the path. Pay attention and you are back in the present moment – the moment of Christ.

Failure and success are not relevant terms to describe your experience of meditation. They are ego terms, and in meditation we are learning to "leave self, the ego, behind." There is no success or failure, only faith: faith active in love.

Whenever the feelings of success or failure arise, simply observe them and remember where they have come from. They will soon subside again and your faith will have been strengthened.

6

The Fruits of Meditation

What "happens" in the actual times of
meditation is not very important. Often, in fact
usually, nothing happens. Like a long plane
journey, you look out of the window and see
clouds, nothing but clouds and blue. Sometimes,
though, it gets bumpy and you fasten your seat
belt and trust the pilot. Sometimes you see the
most beautiful dawn or gorgeous sunset or
staggering displays of light. But what matters is
that you are flying steadily onwards to your
destination. However beautiful or turbulent or
uninteresting the journey, you do not think of
asking the pilot to turn off the engines!

Meditation is not about getting into altered
states of consciousness or seeing and
experiencing anything out of the ordinary. It is
about entering more fully into the ordinary and
discovering thereby the absolute wonder of it,
the presence of God: that the ordinary is shot
through with the extraordinary.

As you grow more steady in keeping your twice daily meditation periods, you will find that the regularity becomes important to the whole balance and peacefulness of each day. If you miss a meditation period, you feel the lack of something essential. Even if your meditation time is turbulent or distracted, it is still the most important part of the day. You are living in a daily discipleship by following so simple a discipline.

An Inner Change

It is in your daily life and especially in your relationships that you will notice the fruits of meditation. Your awareness of this personal inner change may not be rapid or dramatic. It may be reflected to you from those you live and work with. They may remark that you have changed!

The change can best be described in what St. Paul called the "harvest of the Spirit" (Galatians 5:22):

> love, joy, peace, patience, kindness, goodness, fidelity, gentleness and self-control.

Think of each of these qualities in terms of your own personality. You know better than anyone, except the Spirit, which ones you most need.

Notice that love is placed first – the "highest gift." In its path we also find a new joyfulness in life, even in times of stress and suffering.

Joy is deeper than pleasure or happiness. It is found in a new taste for the simple and natural things in life.

Peace is the gift Jesus gives us in his Spirit. It is the energy of his own deep inner harmony with himself, with the Father and with all of creation.

Patience is the cure for our bursts of irritability, rage and intolerance, and all the ways we try to control and possess others.

Kindness is the gift of treating others as we would like them to treat us.

Goodness is not "ours" but we are essentially good, and our human nature is godly because we were created by God and because God lives in us.

Fidelity is the gift that comes through the discipline of the daily meditation and the mantra. For any relationship to be fully human and loving, it is necessary that we deepen it with fidelity.

Gentleness is the practice of non-violence, towards others as well as towards ourselves.

Self-control is necessary if we are to enjoy life in the full liberty of the Spirit. It is the fruit of the balance of meditation, the middle way between all extremes.

"Sinners make the best contemplatives" according to the *Cloud of Unknowing*. This is the heart of the Christian gospel and life: Jesus came to call sinners not the righteous. The fruits of the Spirit grow gradually in us because we begin to turn to the power of love at the centre of our being.

All of these gifts are released as we learn to listen to the language of the heart, which is the silence waiting for us beyond the orbit of our noisy self-fixation.

The source of our being is also the source that heals us and makes us whole. To be whole is to be holy. In meditation we are sanctified in and by the process of being healed.

"Progress": The Journey

John Main called the practice of meditation a
pilgrimage to our own heart. A pilgrimage is a
journey made in the power of the Spirit to a
sacred place. And the most sacred place in the
world is the human heart. We may travel there
alone but we are never alone. The solitude of

meditation cures our most painful loneliness and reveals that we are in a deep and essential relationship.

It is better to think of the journey of meditation as a spiral or a labyrinth rather than as a straight line between two points. That is why the mandala is the universal symbol of the spiritual journey. At times it may seem as though we are going round and round in circles but in fact we are circling in – ever closer to the centre.

The Pilgrim's Labyrinth on the floor of Chartres Cathedral dates from the 13th century. Trace the path from the opening to the centre and you will get a good sense of the journey to the heart we make in meditation. At times frustrating, at times feelings of being lost or wasting time, yet never far from the centre and always circling in nearer and nearer, until you arrive – where you have never ceased to be all the time of the journey while you were on the way. "All the way to heaven is heaven," said St. Catherine of Sienna, "because Jesus is the Way."

An early Christian writer once compared the mystery of God to a circle, whose centre is everywhere and whose circumference is nowhere. Jesus compared the Spirit to the wind which "you cannot tell where it comes from or where it is going." You cannot measure the spiritual. So we do not have to measure or evaluate prayer.

Jesus said he knew where he came from and where he was going. Prayer is a journey into self-knowledge. As we gradually unhook from our selfish self-centredness and egotism, we grow in the knowledge of who we truly are. The "true self" is the most precious value in life because it is our point of meeting with God, and where we are one with God and so with all. Daily meditation is the ordinary process of realising this.

In every journey there are stages, even though, because it is a spiritual journey, we cannot measure them:

1. Conversion

The word conversion means a change of direction. When we first begin to meditate, we may feel the "first fervour" of conversion. The discipline seems easy and we are full of enthusiasm, as in the first stages of a relationship with another person. This initial enthusiasm, of course, will be tested and needs to be deepened by commitment.

2. Uphill

The going can get tough, but in learning to persevere we learn the deep mysteries of God and of our own nature. In the process, there will be times of turbulence when repressed feelings or memories may rise to the surface of our consciousness. This is purifying and liberating but may feel only negative at the time. The support of others at such times is very helpful.

3. Breakthrough

At other times, especially after a prolonged uphill phase, we feel we are breaking through all resistance into a deeper knowledge and love of God, of ourselves and of others. We will then feel a pervasive peace and joy. It is important to accept such times and experiences without trying to possess them, to repeat or manipulate them. Grace means gift. A gift ceases to be a gift when we clutch at it.

The Poor in Spirit

The great quality we learn to reverence as we make this journey is that of poverty.

> Happy are the poor in spirit, theirs is the kingdom of God.
>
> (Matthew 5:3)

If we understand the mantra as our way into poverty, the journey remains a simple one. But simple is not the same as easy. Poverty means letting go: continuously and of everything. Julian of Norwich described it as "A condition of complete simplicity demanding not less than everything." The mantra helps us to fulfil the teaching of Jesus to "leave self behind" and to "abandon all your possessions."

As we meditate day by day, we will find the mantra rooting itself in our heart so that we are able to live the daily round of work and rest with greater awareness of the presence of God. Our lives become more contemplative, that is, more rooted in the present moment, more conscious and more compassionate.

The stages of the inner journey are reflected in the deepening of the mantra and the lessening effort involved in saying it. At first we say the mantra in the face of almost constant distraction. Then we sound the mantra with less effort and are uninterrupted by distractions. Finally we listen to the mantra with a wholeheartedness that takes us beyond the power of distraction altogether.

Of course, the mantra is a discipline, not an end in itself. It is a way to poverty of spirit; it is not the Kingdom itself. There comes a time, then, not in our reckoning, when the mantra will lead us into absolute silence, beyond itself, into the oneness of pure prayer. This is not an experience to be anticipated, imagined or fabricated. When you become aware that you are silent, you should simply resume saying the mantra. If you are conscious of the silence, then of course you are not fully silent; you are thinking, and so you should continue with the mantra.

The guidelines are foolproof if you follow them with real simplicity: say the mantra until you can no longer say it; don't choose when to stop saying it, and start saying it again as soon as you realize that you have stopped.

All these stages of meditation are cyclical as well as progressive. We cover the same ground many times until all the work has been done. The most important thing to remember when we think of progress is that we are, all of us, always simply beginners. Being conscious of that fills life with wonder and liberty. Beginners know best how to give thanks.

Scripture

Meditation greatly enhances the way we read Scripture, and new windows of meaning are opened as the inner experience deepens.

The following passages from the New Testament (New English Bible translation) were especially important to John Main who marked these in his copy. In addition to helping the Christian read the Bible more fruitfully, meditation makes us responsive to the sacred wisdom of the scriptures of other faiths.

St. Matthew's Gospel

Chapter	6	Verses	7-14; 19-21; 33-34
	10		7-8
	13		44-46
	16		24-26
	24		42

St. Mark's Gospel

Chapter	8	Verses	34-36
	10		15

St. Luke's Gospel

Chapter	3	Verses	1-6
	5		16
	6		12
	9		23-24
	12		27-31
	13		18-19
	14		15-24

St. John's Gospel

Chapter	1	Verses	14; 29-34
	3		3-8; 13-17
	4		13-14; 23-24
	5		19-23; 24-26; 39
	6		29; 40; 63; 69
	7		16-18; 28
	8		12; 24; 29-30; 31; 35-36
	10		10
	12		24-26
	13		34-35
	14		2-6; 15-21
	15		5-17
	16		12-14; 33
	17		20-26

Acts of the Apostles

Chapter 2 Verses 32-34
         15   8-9
         17   24-31

St. Paul's Letter to the Romans

Chapter 3 Verses 21-26
         5   1-5
         6   1-11; 13-14; 23
         7   14
         8   4; 9-11; 14-17; 26-30; 38-39
        10   4-10; 11; 14; 17; 20-21
        11   6; 18
        12   1-2
        14   7-12; 15-16
        15   13

St. Paul's First Letter to the Corinthians

Chapter 1 Verses 4-9; 17
         2   1-16
         3   11; 16; 18
         4   20-21
         6   18-20
        10   4-5; 11; 14-17
        13   1-13
        15   20-28; 44-49; 58

St. Paul's Second Letter to the Corinthians

Chapter	1	Verses	19-22
	3		15-18
	4		4-6; 16
	5		2; 14-16; 18
	9		6
	13		4-5

St. Paul's Letter to the Galatians

Chapter	2	Verses	20
	3		26-29
	4		6-7
	5		6; 18; 22-25

St. Paul's Letter to the Ephesians

Chapter	1	Verses	1; 3-10; 17-23
	2		6-7; 12-14; 17-22
	3		4-9; 12-13; 14-21
	4		6-7; 13-14
	5		15-18; 25-33

St. Paul's Letter to the Philippians

Chapter	1	Verses	9-10; 20-21
	2		5
	3		9; 10-11; 21
	4		1; 7

St. Paul's Letter to the Colossians

Chapter	1	Verses	11-20; 26-27
	2		1-5; 6-7; 9-10; 20
	3		4; 9-11
	4		2-3

St. Paul's First Letter to the Thessalonians

Chapter	4	Verse	1

St. Paul's Second Letter to the Thessalonians

Chapter	2	Verses	13-17

St. Paul's First Letter to Timothy

Chapter	4	Verses	9-10
	6		6-7; 15-16

St. Paul's Second Letter to Timothy

Chapter	1	Verses	7-10
	2		1
	3		7

Hebrews

Chapter	6	Verses	1-6
	9		11-14
	10		19-20
	12		28-29

Letter of James

Chapter 3   Verses 13
              5   13-16

First Letter of Peter

Chapter 1   Verses 1; 4; 13-16
              2   1-10; 24
              3   4; 13-16
              4   6; 8

First Letter of St. John

Chapter 2   Verses 24-25; 28-29
              3   14-16; 18; 23-24
              4   7-10
              5   11-12

Further Reading on Meditation

By John Main

The Gethsemani Talks
Word into Silence
Moment of Christ
Letters from the Heart
The Present Christ
The Way of Unknowing
The Heart of Creation
Community of Love
Word Made Flesh
The Inner Christ

By Laurence Freeman

Light Within
The Selfless Self
A Short Span of Days
Common Ground
Jesus: The Teacher Within
*A Pearl of Great Price: Sharing the Gift
    of Meditation by Starting a Group*

By Paul Harris

Christian Meditation by Those Who Practise It
*The Heart of Silence: Contemplative Prayer by
    Those Who Practise It*
John Main: A Biography in Text and Photos
*Frequently Asked Questions About Christian
    Meditation: The Path of Contemplative Prayer*

By Bede Griffiths

The New Creation in Christ

Videos

The Body in Meditation (Mary Stewart and
Giovanni Felicioni)
Christ in the Lotus (An interview with Bede
Griffiths)
Meditation: The Christian Tradition
Coming Home

Audio tapes and videos on Christian Meditation
by John Main, Laurence Freeman and Bede
Griffiths, and others, are also available (for
details, see page 63).

The World Community for Christian Meditation

To communicate and nurture meditation as passed on through the teaching of John Main in the Christian tradition, in the spirit of serving the unity of all.

Life in the dimension of Spirit is a mystery rooted in the joy of being. The wonderful beauty of prayer is that the opening of our heart is as natural as the opening of a flower. To let a flower open and bloom, it is only necessary to let it be, so if we simply are, if we become and remain still and silent, our heart cannot but be open; the Spirit cannot but pour through into our whole being. It is this that we have been created for. In contemplative prayer we seek to become the person we are called to be, not by thinking of God but by being with God. Simply to be with God is to be drawn into being the person God calls us to be.

(John Main)

John Main

John Main (1926-1982) believed that the experience of meditation creates community. His gift was to recover and to re-present a way into this experience for ordinary people from within the Christian contemplative tradition. In the teaching of the Desert Monks on pure prayer he found the practice of the mantra. Realising that this way of prayer could further the search of many modern people for a deeper spiritual life, he recommended two regular daily periods of meditation to be integrated with the usual practices of Christian life.

A way of compassion

Those suffering conflict and division – the great social and psychological distresses of modern society – are called to a deep contemplative response. John Main believed that all human beings, whatever their lifestyle, are called to this contemplative depth.

The meditation group

It is a sign of this vision that meditation groups continue to form around the world. They meet weekly and support each person's own daily commitment to the inner pilgrimage. These groups often make use of the collection of John Main's talks recorded during his teaching of similar groups. Each group is autonomous but linked in a common spirit to the wider community.

The community

The World Community for Christian Meditation was called into being and formed into a flexible structure in 1991. Its aim is to communicate and nurture the teaching of meditation especially through the meditation groups now meeting in homes, parishes, colleges, prisons and communities in about thirty-five countries. Several Christian Meditation Centres participate in this Community, each in its own unique way. The coherence of the community is found in the teaching of John Main, but this only creates a base for a variety of expressions, and new forms of community are encouraged. The link with the monastic tradition, particularly the Benedictine, is highly valued.

The primary responsibilities of the Community, which is served by a Guiding Board, are:

- The annual John Main Seminar, held annually.
- The quarterly *Christian Meditation Newsletter.*
- The Christian Meditation Media publishing company.
- The International Centre in London.

More Information about the Community

If this little book inspires you to begin meditating, you will probably discover the value of sharing the journey with others in this tradition. The most obvious way to do this is to be in touch with one of the regular weekly meditation groups.

If you would like to receive more information about:

• the community, its work and publications

Please contact:

**The World Community
for Christian Meditation
St. Mark's Myddleton Square
London EC1R 1XX
United Kingdom
Tel: + 44 20 7278 2070   Fax: + 44 20 7713 6346
E-mail: mail@wccm.org
Web page: www.wccm.org**

In the United States contact:

The United States National Information Center
627 N. 6th Ave.
Tucson, AZ   85705 (USA)
(520) 882-0290
Toll Free: 1-800-324-8305

Visit The World Community for Christian
Meditation Web site for information, weekly
meditation group readings and discussion at:
www.wccm.org

To obtain a copy of the complete catalog of all
Medio Media meditation material, contact:
Medio Media
627 N. 6th Ave.
Tucson, AZ   85705 (USA)
Toll-free: 1-800-324-8305
E-mail: meditate@mediomedia.org

To order and view the online catalog of all
Medio Media meditation material, visit the
Medio Media Web site: www.mediomedia.org
Toll-free: 1-800-324-8305